CHENILLE OR SILK

Dagger Editions (an imprint of Caitlin Press Inc.)
8100 Alderwood Road,
Halfmoon Bay, BC V0N 1Y1
www.daggereditions.com

Text and cover design by Vici Johnstone
Cover art work: Jacqueline Rush Lee, www.jacquelinerushlee.com
Printed in Canada

Caitlin Press Inc. acknowledges financial support from the Government of
Canada and the Canada Council for the Arts, and the Province of British
Columbia through the British Columbia Arts Council and the Book Publisher's
Tax Credit.

  BRITISH COLUMBIA ARTS COUNCIL Funded by the Government of Canada Canadä

Library and Archives Canada Cataloguing in Publication

McKenna, Emma, 1983-, author

        Chenille or silk / Emma McKenna.

Poems.

ISBN 978-1-987915-89-1 (softcover)

        I. Title.

PS8625.K4245C54 2019   C811'.6   C2018-905974-5

CHENILLE OR SILK

POEMS BY

EMMA MCKENNA

DAGGER EDITIONS

Contents

Chenille or Silk

Snaking	8
Rage Pose	10
Vacation	11
The Mansion	12
Gemini	13
Chenille or Silk	14
Windstorm	16
A Thing of Worth	18
Women's Land	19
May Two-Four	21
Beaubien	22

The Upward Mobility of Tongues

The Upward Mobility of Tongues	24
A Visit with a Prophetess	26
Process	27
Numbers	29
Castle	31
Small Sound	32
Hush Hush	33
Something Integral	35
Chronicle	37
Helms and Moors	39
Currency	41
Traitors	43
Animals	46

Been Healing Since

The Year Everyone Had a Baby   52
The Sylvia Hotel   53
Do You Know Any Science Fiction Poems   55
Familiars   56
Did You Get Enough   57
Coming to Class   59
Greedy   61
Housekeeping   63
One Day   65
Less Partial than Any Other   66
For Anna and Helen, on Twenty Years   67
Fuchsia Waves   68
Boxing Day   69
Been Healing Since   70

Acknowledgements   72

Author Bio   72

CHENILLE OR SILK

SNAKING

Every weekend
We walked through the coolies
Dirt clinging to our canvas shoes
While we tried to keep up
With her quick steps
Ahead of us,
Moving
Stealthily through the shade

The trails
Were long and winding
Underneath railroad tracks
On stilts
That cut boxes into the blue sky
And cast shadows
Like a giant reptile
Across the prairie floor

Up close
We would hold onto the metal poles
Looking up
We thought enviously about the teenagers
Who climbed to the top and threatened to jump
As we swallowed
Dry mouthfuls of wind
Blonde hair whipping against our lips

Cracked, like our courage
As we would wander off the path
Into the elbow-high grass
Yellow and fawn
Stepping carefully
To avoid the holes
A distant rattle
A warning to stand still

Our eyes lock
In hopeful fear
That one of us will get bit
Quick, at the ankle
That one of us
Will suddenly fall in dramatic surrender
Desperately needing the other
To suck the venom from the wound

We have always wandered
Wide-eyed together
Lured forward by the archeology of
A fallen beast's bones
And while I am good
At hearing the hiss and the crack
I have rarely caught
A snake in the grass

Rage Pose

In every instantiation
of my love
the form is shattered.

In folded positions
I access rage
plump, in external hollows.

Pockets that should
be lined with
treasures, instead float

outwards, towards
tile that wraps
around this bath-time scene.

Mimetic
Of what your arms have been.

VACATION

Wouldn't it be nice if I could fold up and disappear
Sometimes?

Oh, not like the anorexic get me smaller
Or I'm in need of women's liberation
Way

I mean—
A simple fold
From here to there
Where I start and you end

"Look, honey,"
I would say
Waning and shifting sideways
Maybe upside down, too
Until I find myself
Completely inside
Myself
With no surface left of you

THE MANSION

There is a scraping sound
Coming up from under the bed

It could be the floorboards
Aching
Or the front door
Opening

I think:
The woman upstairs
Has decided to shovel the front porch

Bent over, in earnest
Proud of her devotion
To this house
To all of us
To something worth pushing for,

Bent over, in the dusk
Metal on concrete
Fighting the urge
To drive her tooth
Through her lip.

GEMINI

You come back
Fish through water
Your transparencies wagging
Mediocre prisms at your side
Propelling you towards me

Oh I am not so foolish
To mistake colour for substance
Or gills for security
But the slippery promise of pleasure
Threatens to hook me by the lip

I know by now
That all you can give me
Is the music of little bones breaking
As you flip back and forth
Caught on your precious pain

Take your breath
And put it to good use
Gasp, sputter, moan
I refuse to hold my hand out
For too much salt and thin skin.

CHENILLE OR SILK

Dad,
I can see you chewing
a million miles away
inside my head.

And you have this grin on
so tight across your little
teeth
it's almost vulgar.

I want to shift the guilt
I feel tonight
Sleeping for free again
on someone else's mattress

I want to shift the weight
again
from me to you
because you look too comfortable—

And I'm squirming
in the luxury I am copying
since I am opting for adoption
at the least, through marriage

If I am someone's wife
will it matter that I am nobody's daughter?

Who would let their child
paint her body like that
all coloured and exclamation
marked

Somebody should have thrown
a blanket over me sooner

something chenille or silk
to cover up the dirt

Listen.
I am getting
older
again this year.

Each year
a little more safe inside this body
lessening
the space you take up.

With a lot of practice
I have begun to fill
the holes with sky,
the distance with trust.

WINDSTORM

my mother called this morning to warn me
There is a windstorm in Toronto
the news must have said
and she dialled my number
to tell me—
not to walk down the streets
with the flying debris
while my windowpane
has been shaking since dawn
a cold draft crawling under my covers
curling up under my arms

last night I saw on the news
that two sisters
eleven and thirteen
went missing in Oshawa,
from two separate group homes
I went cold all over
like a deep breath had hauled itself up my back

that might have been us,
me and my sister,
at twelve and fifteen
holding mittened hands
jumping into a snow-capped river
or taking too many pills behind a liquor store
with freshly penned notes
to no one
left on the ice and the white lines
in some parking lot
in some town

but maybe they are still alive
and just running
did they save up their seven-dollar-a-week allowances
to purchase one-way Greyhound tickets

back, to the prairies
or north to Montreal
to become blonde or exotic

did they fill their backpacks
with their old t-shirts and jeans
and duck out to a friend's house
to hide behind dry weed and fresh poems

we were barely adolescent
when we hauled that leather suitcase up,
from the basement and out of the front door
what did we even put in it?
I don't remember packing
I only remember
clutching you, sobbing

in the hollow space
between the two columns of townhouses
the snow had already turned to ice under our boots
as we shifted our weight
back and forth
wiping our tears and laughing
trying to decide where to go

as if leaving home
were an adventure we could get right
and the wind
tore through us
that mid-January night
while our mother
sat stiffly on the other side of that wall
breathing in her pride
and I want to know—
was she scared for me then?
I was, I was.

A Thing of Worth

Why consider
the perfect stanza
when illness is expanding
in every opening

It is a Saturday
so I try to listen:
there are voices in the alley
there is garbage being sorted

There is an entire economy
of lost and found
circulating behind me—
have I discarded a thing of worth?

A quarrel has broken out
bottles in carts
rumble at one another
she breaks, between singing

And hollering at a man
I project "partners" onto them
demanding even of strangers
some semblance of monogamy

Your promise ring
cold against my breast
I gloat to the winter afternoon
lonely, but loved, too

Women's Land

the land within you
won't compromise
so you expand and expand

but we are all trying
and trailing behind you
you show me places where you have

cleared the bush
and levelled the dirt
flagging off zones for chairs and canopies

we both know
the work belongs to the Latino gardener
but the property, the property belongs to you

you have pruned
the greatest of these trees
and so we suck on plums together

pulling their ripe bodies
off the branches
chafed between links of barbed wire

then you ask me:
Do you like animals?
Yes, wild ones, I answer, thinking of the deer

Huh:
you respond with boredom
as I have again said the Wrong Thing

since I have arrived
in this pastel blue and pink fantasy
I have been made aware of my deficits

your child
our only commonality,
has become a commodity between us

but inside that freckled indigo
is a love for us both
and you can't meditate me out

MAY TWO-FOUR

Last year
It was her and I
And the fireworks wouldn't stop for nobody

At night
We wore extra tights
And envied our friends' wool sweaters

In the day
We crept brave
And bumpy skin from the sauna to the lake

It was new
We no longer played
At grown up love but lived it with our bodies

Those shapes
We tucked into one another
Sheepish and ashamed at our own dimensions

But change
It happens quickly
Inserts her fingers and hooks them in

She bought
Fat-feather pillows
And threw out my last flat one some afternoon

My neck
Began to grow
Crooked with the effort of watching her

Tonight
There are exploded cartridges
Littering the street outside of our old apartment

I still hear
The sound of the road
While in the back seat she sighed beside me

BEAUBIEN

In the middle of the highway
on my way to your city, the road is split;
I watch purple- and maroon-crowned reeds bending in succession

Leaning and reaching out to nothing
but the space between one another, arching forward,
past the seat in front of me, I pretend my breath is what pushes them

Those men stacking iron
beneath the underpass in orange vests and hard hats
must have some part to play in the way the forest is dividing

This late August afternoon
I will find my way to your street, to again lay
against your chest, your great arms sprawled behind you

Of all the things you've seen
I want to give to you nothing heavier than this:
an image of dancing reeds, noticing, now, how it moved me.

THE UPWARD MOBILITY OF TONGUES

THE UPWARD MOBILITY OF TONGUES

How different would we look
if we had always
had
enough to eat?

Whiter teeth, for sure, more
entitled
to take up space
in the gape of our face

Less frantic,
unlikely to rise up out of bed
a flesh storm of want and greed
filling the bowels with a lover's refuse

But maybe just as hungry,
you never know.

Aren't all teeth
capable
of the same embellished grind?

You would think
(not *you*, but *them*)
that value
has gone up;

inflation of the page
making words
multi-dimensional
giving meaning
to the upward

            mobility
                      of
tongues

as   if   we   were   weightless   all   along

See:
        skinny is a state of mind.

A Visit with a Prophetess

My sadness
Is a gulp that pulls
Every thought and motivation
Down the back of my throat
A choke that harnesses me

I wonder
Do you know the route
From my grief to my longing
Can you pry my mouth
Into a moan

It isn't the sound
But the outline it makes
When it hits the walls
These walls that push back
Against me

A prophetess
Could warn us
That swallowing one another
Whole, will only lead to
Emptiness

The spit in the gut
Like a worm in a hollow
Full and flexing
With the glimmer
Of its own secretion

I envy
Your calm
And I wonder,
Do you know the way
Out of here?

PROCESS

1.

It's that same fear every time
like wolves howling up the spine

The first attempt:
get the bodies down
at least the skeleton on the ground

Tip
the glacier that says
"You Can't."

Nothing falls across this back
shelved thoughts
storm out to undo the loss.

2.

Put your finger
on the feeling you had

the one where the words
jumped
and you caught them
slumped and sliding

the letter,
the fleck,
that threatens to come off

If I rub
the spot where
my emotions seeped through
will the page be more committal?
Come on
Put your finger on the spot

where theory shifted into sighs
and skin prickled with the closeness of
words
that sounded out as if they always knew
you

But remember
she read it, too.

NUMBERS

exalt
in numbers
that feel sharp and pointed
in my direction

or outwards, really
horizon beckoning

encapsulated in joy
I jump
onto the bed
to congratulate me
through you

Dancing across the room
my feet are learning
Timeless

You know how hard this has been on me
the waking up with
that process laid out above me

"Fit me into this"
somewhere
or is it really
about removal

I am fuelled by creation:
I want to generate
thoughts like women
opining for babies

Blood soaked and nutrient rich
little beady eyes to stare into
thinking, "It looks just like me"

Thinking;
How can they, with their skin dragged down by the gravity of longing,
The endless work of provisions

Peeling back our dreams to try and get deeper/
into

the core
inaccessible
except by your hands
and my fervour

The Creating Kind.

The: "I need to make this before it makes me—"
Happy?

No, slut, happen.

CASTLE

I once could imagine
that I would be capable
of building myself into a castle
limb by limb
my arms would extend above me
pillars of knowledge
Like:
"I know I am right"
and
"I deserve love"

but look at the moat
that trails from my legs
does that seem like
anything pure to you?

It's true I have kept my elbows and knees shackled
It's true I have sworn to bend to you again

But what of all the little fires
you have started?

It feels impossible to move
and I worry
that every corner I can't see
is about to burst into flames.

SMALL SOUND

trapped in the trap in me
is a small sound
like a bird being smothered
a child being murdered
a glass being shattered

it is the cliché of all the clichés I swallowed to convince myself that I could
love you
it is the force of all the wind I backed against to try and resist you
it is the weight of all the times you have laid on top of me

oh little sound
can you give me a flicker
of promise that you will shut up again?

Can you:
Break your own beak
Slit your own throat
Crack your own bones

I would give you all the words I have gathered
like, "sorry" and "please" and "stay"
I would give them to you to hold onto
or better yet, to place discreetly under your pillow

Remember:
When I wrote you heart-shaped love notes and tucked them in your
clothes before you went away?
Why didn't that work
        to preserve you.

Hush Hush

there is something incredible
that commands me
to wake up

and put these jeans on;
buttons, clasps and dials

all morning
there are dozens of tasks

and I
would be lost in it all—
        a smear
        of mascara
        dragged through
        last night's tears
—if not for these structures
of cloth
that bind me to this body
a thing,

I would so rather leave behind

the endless chore of keeping it propped up
exhausts even the powder
I dust on to cover me

every gesture
an attempt
to make the me "ME" better.

I counted, all day
for this moment
        when I could return
        to weightless grief

      your guilt, corpse-like, at my back
instead I feel jealous
of the wave I gave
to an old crush

she just jumped out of my fingertips
stripped and ready
to incite

I should bury the hush hush
plunge those fingers down my throat
"zip it up"

because the most pleasure I can expect
is in the vault of the shower
in the steady drum of
acceptance.

Something Integral

my whole body is clenched up like my stomach
imitating its contortions
acting like
the centre of some sick show

this room is a vista
a come-to or come-through
kind of place
where we go to get away

but where can I direct this tension
when you are so innocent, so repetitively unexposed
I see you, in moments
as a child I didn't have

I want the masculinity in you
the coercive and knowing
struggle to break me to break you
you, your

butchness, with the jaunty
swagger and the out-turned
knees, cradling me in your
fist

suddenly, I got too old
for something integral,
watching this game that is tired
of us both

I keep laying back
and looking up at you
desperate to fix the need
in me

tell me: if I should give up
on this fight for
my desire,
will there

be a more romantic
room, to spill myself into;
will I ever get closer
to golden?

CHRONICLE

I yearn to write about
Triumph

But it falls so completely
To the other side

When the pulp of anxiety
Pulls through.

The upward lean
Of nourishment

Blocking out the twist
Each tulip

Prompts her own mouth
Upward

To burst through the scented
Room

A chronicle, of her new
Despair.

The blinds hammer down
Ferociously

Edges chattering against
The cold

Further in here, where
The radiator

Mumbles, I will stand
Up

And let this womb, hang
Envelope-like

From these words, promising
Nothing

But the creak of another
Evening

Hunched out, back spread
To the door

Or the wall, if I change
My direction.

HELMS AND MOORS

what is a helm,
really,
and where should I find one?

in the living room/
the sitting room/
the rec room/
        near the mantle?

close to something constructed
that juts out
        chin-like
from the bank in the wall

is it similar to the Grimaldi?
        nestled so quietly
        in the surface of the moon
        it took us centuries to notice it

so how can it be expected
that I could find one, here?

when I am hemmed in
by conventions and the constant pulse of
that love

it should call me
forth
and returning
like a voice on the moors

rich with the texture of a greenery
so close to the skin

like wool/
it would/
hem me in

if only I knew
how to recognize it.

CURRENCY

trying to talk about money
is like expounding this landscape

to you
there are:
      corners
      where roofs meet frames

      wheels
      appended to metal

      a branch
      leaping from its shadow

would a teller have another version?
a vision rounded first into acknowledgement and then sharpened by the sound

thousands of leaves clapping
for the returning surf

I can't help but feel as if the canoe
sunk against the one-inch tree
has really fallen
      as if, her arms were by her side
      to protect the curves
      of her centre
      a rusted mummy
      probably, still useful

there is a chance
it will recreate itself
that the water will replenish
and drag that old body back to work

is work so bad, you say, as if it were only an Idea
and of all the little things
you consider relevant

the current—
its direction and shape, or maybe is it the smell?—
is hardly one of them

TRAITORS

Don't tell them
your wrist hurts
from pressing down—

they'll ask to see
your fingertips
for signs of where
you dared to spell
your name.

They will ask
if the bathroom stall or
high-school hall
deserved
what you did.

You can shake your head
no
now
because they like to talk about justice
but no one deserves—

Don't tell me
your hands hurt
from cleaning the house

      with comet and pine-sol and windex and murphy oil, for the wood

I'll ask to smell
your fingertips
for signs of cigarettes
you are a little bitch;
a traitor, who should know better.

Who should know better?

I have to tell you
even though my fingers hurt
from writing
poem upon poem/
about her/

She hand-wrote every essay in university
bent over the kitchen table late into the night

smoke,
curling up around her
as if it were a veil of protection.
Shaking her head,
no

> *I know better*
> *than to think*
> *I will escape*
> *with a million words*
> *pushed out*

And somewhere up north
she is again,
writing
though she grips the pen
less in defence, now.

Finally
quiet enough
in her trailer
to rework sounds of love
onto the page.

Lately, we dance carefully
over the years
favouring the first few
and lately, together
can admire her courage—

Just don't tell me
that I hurt you
unless you have

somewhere else to go.

ANIMALS

1.

When we are reduced/
we are reduced
to animals.

Curled up on the floor
an island towel in a
linoleum ocean

you are flooded
with someone else's
blood

and I begged of you
breathing through you
breath, wrapped, around you

to carry on;
and if you needed to
let go/ and I would still hold you.

2.

animals
don't talk with dollar bills in their teeth

they love
with the raw estimate of

how
close
can
I
get

to leave him now
would be to

euthanize
a part of us
an extra limb
we've tacked on
to make loving feel
bigger

and I want to be
bigger

so sick of dollars
trying to turn me into
the small child

I think I was?

it's always money money money with you
But it's money talking, too.

3.

look at you:
so carefree
you are everything He never was

there is
something truthful
in the disparaging of the maternal

the way
he responds
to you, like a friend without betrayal

so unlike
the suspicion
he turns on me, unless my hand

is filled
with food
too tentative to actually touch

with some
honest submission
just the harshness of a slap

and the
performative touch
of a woman who knows

she is
being watched
with steady eyes of gold

turned upwards,
is her love the kind
worth sticking it out for?

4.

now I
know, I should never have let you see The Real
Me

the dancing
wagging head on the floor, breasts rolling to the
ceiling

you believe
in the curve of my calves, the way they have
softened

I stopped
running when I met you, I pulled my bones
down

to buckle
my skin in a quieter procession, still
wild

with loss
and gravid with promise, the rest
shook

from infinite
patterns of desire and plenitude, out of these
hands

a logic
unfolds and drapes us in violet, and nothing
since

has resonated
like my gloating, the way my mouth rises to enclose
you.

BEEN HEALING SINCE

The Year Everyone Had a Baby

The year everyone had a baby
blonde-bobbed before me
my own belly ached

Those women who are horse faced
have always run faster
smelling cold and clean

Wearing uniforms of workers
Factory-pressed squares
one size fits most

Before you start to think I'm barren
realize I have these
twins of my own

Envy and Contempt
competing for attention
bad at keeping friends

Sure—sometimes I abort them
over and over again
before they can even talk

More often, I give them life
let them take shape, grow
have a soul or, whatever

There is no measurement
of what makes
a woman good

Laughing widely, they always say
Go on, figure it out
for yourself

The Sylvia Hotel

I went all the way to Vancouver
Only to come home again

And I woke up there,
That first morning, reeling.

I didn't exactly sight-see
But a few things jumped out

Between me and my memories
Unsettling the unrelenting rain

Like the place where our old dog would run
In circles, or nose garbage, annoyed

Yeah, before he got so sick
I found him crumpled up on the carpet

But this time, I came with a different creature
We stayed close to the water

Transfixed less by the glisten
Than by the garish condo advancing

Above us, lit up all night
Tableaux of the rich in their bathrooms

Once, two floors below I watched
Thinking of how far I was from

A woman in an apron making
A thing to proudly eat

My days remained, broken up
By meals I anxiously worked through

It took hours to get it all in
And by nightfall I was wired

Into some reality show
While he laughed larger than his mouth

I rested on edge between full
Absorption and distraction

Should I count everything?
Or let it all blur, into nothing

I can't (one)
I can't (two)
I can't (three)

But somehow I am—
          still
managing.

My therapist repeats that the improvements
Are incremental

But I want to count that up, too
Hungry for proof

That I can get back there
To that place I had finally found

Where the spider plants are still dying
Still pretending to be green

And where, he is often beside me
Reminding me that here is good.

Do You Know Any Science Fiction Poems

Do you know any science fiction poems?

Tonight, when we are in bed,
can you recite for me
lyrics of a future
I want words hard and square
to box me in
create corners behind my eyes
you can explain the rotation
of moons
or the descent and shadow
of a planet
that has lost its place

the more mundane
the better
let the words, glowing yellow now,
rest like beams above me
your voice
the pull of a gravity
so close to the surface
of sleep

with you,
I can sink into darkness
while your hand
rests coolly
on my back.

FAMILIARS

Has it been sweet to you.

It depends
where on the tongue
you place it.

I put out the call
but no one familiar has answered.

Did I forget to mention
my own name
so charged with regret
and ego
and go

get the remains of my betrayals
and build them an altar
light a candle for each one
and spell out
forgiveness.

One letter at a time
is not enough to absolve this.

There is tenderness in the afterglow
in that moment before it is suddenly dark

let that second span out
cover me, and

promise me this: you will leave my dreams alone. Let's meet on the corner,
in the daylight, and compare who has shifted shapes, after all.

Did You Get Enough

The last time I saw my father
I was skinny
SKINNY
(s k i n n y)
and I wore high-heeled boots that clicked.

But that had no purchase on him
he was only
interested
in the
Idea of Daughter.

Between full cheeks
I spared him
rage
unswallowed
for eighteen years

and asked him,
only some of my questions

my mouth, working
for the whole of Us

and he answered
only some of my questions

Still he insisted
I should call him Dad
the word, hard
a well-worn stone
lodged in a child's throat.

I suppose
since then

he has changed his phone number,
again. But I kind of remember
where he lives—

His house,
hanging onto the side of a cliff
my cheekbones
ragged, reaching
towards my father's eyes

When all he wants to know is,
pushing
back
his chair from the table,
did you get enough?

COMING TO CLASS

Oh look she's coming to class
Come on, how'd you get like that
Eating donut holes
Watching tv all afternoon with the curtains drawn
Up close to the women
The beige carpet under your nose
While your mother is out working
And your baby brother crawls

Oh no she's coming to class
Tell us, how'd you get like that
Eating foodbank donuts
Frozen and defrosted
Cutting your own hair
Screaming under the faucet
Getting stuffed in a locker
Buried in dirt while recess goes on around you

Oh well she's coming to class
Show us, how'd you get like that
Eating day old donuts
Sprawled on a table
Sweat soaked old black shirts
Ketamine coated nostril
Orange stained fingertips
And the ghost of weed always on your lips

Oh okay she's coming to class
Prove it, how'd you get like that
Eating gluten free dairy free never free treats
Vegetables grains and protein
Diarrhea in the morning
Attaching notes to quotes
Drawers lined with debts and dignity
Tattoing your arm with the word *destiny*

So what I've been coming to
Coming to
Coming to
Class
Trying to tell you how I got like that
Coming up on nothing
Standing here like a teacher's pose
At least a teacher knows
Something

GREEDY

I am jealous
of poets

reconfiguring their faces
escapes, resentments
into clean lines
whorls of saliva
glistening and groping
become corners
numbered
edited.

I am jealous
of dancers

twisting their bodies
angles, grief
into strikes
of desire
limbs resolving into steps
leapt
crouched
lifted.

I am jealous
of painters

enlarging their eyes
circling, borders
into glances
cast downward, resin seeping
through colours
trailing
softened
imagined.

I am greedy
for poems,
running clear and quick
for dances,
shaping skin into air
for paintings,
fixing figures in flight.

Housekeeping

You look like yoga
More comfortable
Than we have ever been
You walk with ease
And even your laugh
Sounds spotless.

I can't make out
A thing you say
I'm so distracted
With counting up
The rooms I can hear
Echoing in your complaints.

Do you have a
Housekeeper yet
It doesn't matter much
If it's now or soon
It's that inevitable way
You told me, *you're impossible.*

Funny how
It's me, flattened out
Spine twisting
Feeling guilty
For all the useless
Objects.

I was shocked that
First time I climbed
Stairs cleaned by a woman
Living in another
House, her face,
Unknown.

I am still ashamed that
Once I snapped
At the housekeeper
When I was working
As a nanny, both of us,
Competing for privacy.

But I was
Paid more, owned more
Allowed more,
Lamenting this now
This soundless
Apology.

Funny how
I still think of you
While I stretch
Towards the west
Focusing on the
Possible.

One Day

One day you will live,
and you will live in a room,
a room with peaceful things.

And you will be allowed,
to just be there,
in all of your ways,
and just notice.

Less Partial than Any Other

You, who would love me with my original teeth
twisted, crooked, bent, cluttered
distorting my mouth
my cheeks fallen in shame around them
my chin, defiant.

You, who would love me with my original skin
slit, stretched, stabbed, scabbed
displaying my wounds
my muscles pushing through with strength
my scars, radiant.

You, who would love me with my original heart
cowering, eager, biting, covering
deforming my hope
my regrets roiling and racing
my fear, reproducing.

You, who would love me now
after all I have amassed
and shed.
Still, that original girl.
You, who sees me, finally,
less partial than any
other.

For Anna and Helen, on Twenty Years

We came to you
Ragged, unravelled, enraged
Looking for something temporary
To offset the permanence of all this non-belonging
How many of us have you held
Between your love?

We came to you
Curious, uncertain, entitled
Navigating the idea of property
And propriety and the luxury of naming as mine
How many of us have you housed
Between your love?

We came to you
Questioning, determined, yearning
Awestruck at the compassion
You have placed at the base for your nourishment
How many of us have you supported
Between your love?

I came to you
Nine years ago, cracked right through
With grief and longing
I circle back now, to see you
To learn from you, to honour you
How many times have you held me, housed me, and supported me,
Between your love?

What a capacious love,
To invite us all in to witness it,
Knowing that we will always take
Some of you with us
When we do finally leave.

Fuchsia Waves

Once you unwrap the word
Rape

It is hard to find a place to put it

The body says it doesn't belong
Here

While it clutches to fuchsia waves

The mind outlines each letter in
Memory

But its ink is watery and translucent

And the heart, well, it is nothing if not
Predictable

Preferring to beat you with adrenaline

Lining the mouth with a sour tasting
Truth

As you say it over and over again

Weeks minutes and years and maybe
Later

      You will stare at its harsh corners

      You will examine its thick content

      You will brush against its cool surface

      You will learn its silhouette a sometimes shadow

Finding ways to move within it

BOXING DAY

Throw out all your old nail polish
as if you recently learned it's toxic

grow up, act twelve again
tie that tiffany-blue bow in your hair

postpone deoderant
last year's onesie all day

sort the gifts into piles
to keep or to give away

text all the mothers
remind them that you're grateful.

BEEN HEALING SINCE

Been healing since
conception/
that originary trauma

when he and you
found me
maybe,
you fought
        for me
to be born to
to grow into
to get to
name
the sounds
you thought were
in your mind

holding my breath
on the phone
I tell you
in one word
how I'm hurting
and
how I'm proud of you

I can be both
I can be many
and we are never just one thing
just this chain of
        feeling
emerging as
the flash of eyes
the cramming of teeth
the laughter
I welcome

I   inhale

say prayers
to some universal
not only "woman"
but,
wanting,
working,
willing,
a different cycle
that takes less.

Why is it that
the broken
are expected to stay
fragmented?
I don't want to be the bearer of that
burden, anymore

besides,
I need to be ready
for the opportunity
        to carry my grandmother
        to cradle my mother
        to comfort my sister
because we've all been lifting since birth.

Acknowledgements

Thank you to the wonderful team at Dagger Editions and Caitlin Press for believing in this book and making it possible.

To the women in my life, whose friendship has inspired, challenged and sustained me.

To my siblings, who are the origins and endings of all of my most important stories.

And to my partner, for the bright circle he has drawn around my days.

Photo Carly Spoelstra

Emma McKenna is a multidisciplinary writer and scholar. Her previous work as a musician includes the LP *Run with It* and digital EPs *The Might* and *What It Becomes*. Emma holds a PhD in English and cultural studies (ABD, McMaster University), and is an educator on social justice, intersectional feminism and sexuality studies. Emma's academic writing can be found in *Hypatia: A Journal of Feminist Philosophy*, *Women: A Cultural Review*, *Atlantis: Critical Studies in Gender, Culture and Social Justice* and *Review of Education, Pedagogy, and Cultural Studies*. Emma lives with her partner in Hamilton, Ontario. *Chenille or Silk* is her first book.